ABT

ALLEN COUNTY PUBLIC LIBRARY

FRIEN W9-AEG-380

OF ACPL

THE
MEDICAL
ZONE

Jokes, Riddles, Tongue Twisters & "Daffynitions"

By Gary Chmielewski

Illustrated by Jim Caputo

Read Jokes. Write Jokes.

NORWOODHOUSE PRESS

A Note to Parents and Caregivers:

As the old saying goes, "Laughter is the best medicine." It's true for reading as well. Kids naturally love humor, so why not look to their interests to get them motivated to read? The Funny Zone series features books that include jokes, riddles, word plays, and tongue twisters—all of which are sure to delight your young reader.

We invite you to share this book with your child, taking turns to read aloud to one another, practicing timing, emphasis, and expression. You and your child can deliver the jokes in a natural voice, or have fun creating character voices and exaggerating funny words. Be sure to pause often to make sure your child understands the jokes. Talk about what you are reading and use this opportunity to explore new vocabulary words and ideas. Reading aloud can help your child build confidence in reading.

Along with being fun and motivating, humorous text involves higher order thinking skills that support comprehension. Jokes, riddles, and word plays require us to explore the creative use of language, develop word and sound recognition, and expand vocabulary.

At the end of the book there are activities to help your child develop writing skills. These activities tap your child's creativity by exploring numerous types of humor. Children who write materials based on the activities are encouraged to send them to Norwood House Press for publication on our website or in future books. Please see page 24 for details.

Above all, the most important part of the reading experience is to have fun and enjoy it!

Sincerely,

Shannon Cannon

Shannon Cannon
Literacy Consultant

NORWOOD HOUSE PRESS

P.O. Box 316598 • Chicago, Illinois 60631
For information regarding Norwood House Press, please visit our website at: www.norwoodhousepress.com or call 866-565-2900.

Copyright © 2009 by Norwood House Press.
All rights reserved. No part of this book may be reproduced or utilized in any form or by any means without written permission from the publisher.

Editor: Jessy McCulloch
Designer: Design Lab

Library of Congress Cataloging-in-Publication Data:
Chmielewski, Gary, 1946–
  The medical zone / by Gary Chmielewski ; illustrated by Jim Caputo.
    p. cm. — (The funny zone)
  Summary: "Book contains 100 medical-themed jokes, tongue twisters and "Daffynitions". Backmatter includes creative writing information and exercises. After completing the exercises, the reader is encouraged to write their own jokes and submit them for web site posting and future Funny Zone editions. Full-color illustrations throughout"—Provided by publisher.
  ISBN-13: 978-1-59953-299-8 (library edition : alk. paper)
  ISBN-10: 1-59953-299-9 (library edition : alk. paper) 1.
Medicine—Juvenile humor. I. Caputo, Jim. II. Title.
  PN6231.M4C46 2009
  818'.5402—dc22   2008035197

Manufactured in the United States of America

OOPS!

How do you avoid that rundown feeling?
Look both ways before you cross the street in traffic!

"Doctor, I've broken my arm in two places."
"Well don't go back to either one!"

"Doctor, I dropped a bowling ball on my foot."
"That's just *swell*!"

Patient: "Doctor, I swallowed a bone."
Doctor: "Are you choking?"
Patient: "No, really I did!"

Why do some people get all the breaks?
They're clumsy!

OFFICE TIME

Why did the Gingerbread Man go to the doctor?
He felt *crummy*!

"Doctor, you have to help me out."
"Certainly. Which way did you come in?"

Why did the ham go to see a doctor?
It wanted to know if it could be *cured*!

Doctor: "How do you know you have upside-down disease?"
Patient: "My nose runs and my feet smell!"

Do doctors make house calls?
Yes, but the house has to be really sick!

Doctor: "Good afternoon, Ms. Salerno, I haven't seen you for a long time."
"I know, I've been ill," she replied.

"Doctor, I'm here for my heart."
"Sorry, I don't have it!"

Doctor: "Don't you know that my hours are from 1pm to 3pm?"
Joe: "Yes, but the dog that bit me doesn't!"

Why did the clown go to the doctor?
He was feeling a little funny!

"You see, Doctor, I'm always dizzy for half an hour after I get up in the morning."
"Well, try getting up a half an hour later!"

A patient went to the family doctor and asked, "Will you give me something for my leg?"
"Well, I don't need it right now, but I can offer you $1 if you're desperate," he replied.

Keith: "I've got a nasty pain in my left foot."
Doctor: "You shouldn't worry – it's just old age."
Keith: "Well – then why doesn't the other one hurt? I've had that just as long."

Patient: "My head feels like iron, my neck is stiff, and my sinuses won't drain."
Doctor: "You don't need a doctor, you need a plumber!"

Why didn't the girl go to the doctor after she swallowed a clock?
She didn't want to alarm everybody!

Doctor: "I've given you a thorough exam and all you need is rest."
Laura: "But, I feel sick. Why don't you look at my tongue?"
Doctor: "That needs a rest too."

"Doctor, ever since I've been riding in the rodeo, I haven't been feeling well. What do you think it could be?"
"**Bronc**-itis!"

"Doctor, I just can't seem to shake this cold. I spent the last seven days in bed and I feel drained."
"Well, that's the problem. Don't you know that seven days in bed make one *weak*!"

Maria: "Doctor, I'm seeing double."
Doctor: "Take a seat. I'll be with you shortly."
Maria: "Which one?"

Wayne: "Doctor, you're a genius. You've cured my hearing problem."
Doctor: "Good. That'll be $100."
Wayne: "What did you say?"

Why did the pillow go to the doctor?
It was feeling all stuffed up!

Doctor: "I have good news and bad news about your condition. Which do you want first?"
Brian: "The good news."
Doctor: "The good news is that you have 24 hours to live."
Brian: "If that's the good news, what's the bad news?"
Doctor: "I should have told you yesterday!"

AN APPLE A DAY

Show me a diet doctor and I'll show you someone who lives off the fat of the land!

Which state has the most doctors?
MD

What was the doctor's advice for the train conductor while eating?
Chew, chew!

Did you hear about the doctor who performed surgery by correspondence?
He's being sued for mail-practice!

How do doctors deal with amnesia patients?
They make them pay in advance!

Tannia: "Why are you eating your dinner on the side of the street?"
Lisa: "The doctor told me to curb my appetite!"

Why don't doctors predict who will get measles?
They don't want to make *rash* decisions!

How long should a doctor practice medicine?
Until he gets it right!

Why did the house call the doctor?
It had window *panes*!

What do you call a group trip for physicians?
A doc-tour!

When do doctors get angry?
When they run out of *patients*!

THE CURE

Doctor: "Keep taking your medicine and you'll live to be 100."
Elmer: "Doc, I'll be 100 on Wednesday."
Doctor: "In that case, you can stop taking the medicine on Tuesday!"

What's the difference between a hill and a pill?
One is hard to get up and the other hard to get down!

Chase: "Why are you jumping up and down?
Jessy: "I've just taken some medicine and forgot to shake the bottle!"

What's the most dangerous part of a needle?
The end!

Doctor: "Have you been taking those memory pills I gave you?"
Kathleen: "No, I forgot!"

Michael: "Doctor, these pills you gave me for body odor are of no use."
Doctor: "What's wrong with them?"
Michael: "They keep slipping from under my arms!"

Sarah: "I still feel very tired, Doctor."
Doctor: "Didn't you take those sleeping pills I gave you?"
Sarah: "Well, they looked so peaceful in the little bottle that I didn't want to wake them!"

Kevin: "What's wrong, sis?"
Jade: "The doctor gave me some medicine and told me to take three teaspoons a day."
Kevin: "So?"
Jade: "I only have two teaspoons!"

11

DOCTOR, DOCTOR!

"Doctor, I've just swallowed the film from my camera."
"Let's hope nothing develops!"

"Doctor, have you got something for a bad headache?"
"Of course. Take this hammer and hit yourself on the head – then you'll have a bad headache!"

"Doctor, I snore so loud I keep myself awake."
"Sleep in another room!"

"Doctor, I keep thinking there's two of me."
"One at a time please!"

"Doctor, I feel like a king."
"What's your name?"
"Joe."
"You must be Joe King!"

"Doctor, I think I'm a goat."
"How long have you felt like this?"
"Since I was a kid!"

"Doctor, my tongue is all red."
"Take it back to the library!"

"Doctor, I keep stealing things."
"Have you taken anything for it?"

"Doctor, I keep seeing into the future."
"When did this first happen?"
"Next Wednesday!"

"Doctor, I feel funny today.
What should I do?"
"Become a clown!"

"Doctor, you've got to help me.
Everyone thinks I'm a liar."
"I can't believe that!"

"Doctor, my head
feels funny."
"So don't touch it!"

"Doctor, my throat is sore."
"So why don't you apologize to it?"

"Doctor, can I have a second opinion?"
"Of course, come back tomorrow!"

"Doctor, I have a terrible migraine."
"It's all in your head!"

"Doctor, I need help. I can
never remember what I just said."
"When did you first notice this problem?"
"What problem?"

"Doctor, I dream there are monsters
under my bed. What can I do?"
"Saw the legs off!"

CHECKING IN

What did the doctor say to her patient after she finished the operation?
"That's enough out of you!"

Patient: "What did they find when they X-rayed my brain?"
Doctor: "Nothing!"

SPACE FOR RENT

Would you survive if they cut off your left side?
You'll be *all right*!

Why are anesthesiologists good at math?
Because of all the **numb**-ers!

Which doctor is a real knockout?
An anesthesiologist!

Two girls were born in the same hospital on the same day. They have the same father and mother, but they are not twins. How can this be?
They are two of a set of triplets!

Why do surgeons wear masks during operations?
If they make a mistake, no one will know who did it!

Do pneumonia patients make quick recoveries?
No, it takes them a lung, lung time!

When they take out an appendix, it's an appendectomy; and when they remove your tonsils, it's a tonsillectomy. What's it called when they remove a growth from your head?
A haircut!

What did one tonsil say to the other tonsil?
"Time to get up! The doctor is taking us out!"

Doctor: "Don't worry, after the operation you'll be a new man."
Devin: "That's great! Could you send the bill to the old man?"

15

Why did the doctor move the patient away from the windows?
So she would feel no *pane*!

Why is the doctor so dizzy?
He just finished making the rounds!

What happened when the doctor told a joke during surgery?
She left her patient in stitches!

What's a surgeon's favorite musical?
Phantom of the **Opera**-tion!

Carol: "Doctor, I'm scared. This is my first operation."
Doctor: "I know how you feel Carol. You are my first patient!"

What plant grows in a hospital room?
An *IV*!

What kind of dog do you find in a hospital?
A doc-shund!

Doctor: "How are you doing after your heart operation, Mr. Delgado?"
Mr. Delgado: "Well, Doctor, I'm fine, but I seem to have two heartbeats."
Doctor: "Oh. I always wondered where my wristwatch went."

Why did the doctor operate on her medical book?
To take out its *appendix*!

NEWS FLASH – A man walked into the hospital asking for a brain operation. Fortunately, the doctors were able to change his mind.

THE NURSE KNOWS BEST

Nine nice night nurses nursing nicely.

Nurse: "Can I take your pulse?"
Tony: "Why, haven't you got one of your own?"

Surgeon: "Nurse, did you put the patient to sleep?"
Nurse: "Yes, I just told her some of these jokes!"

Nurse: "May I dress your cut?"
Frank: "Why, don't you like what it's wearing?"

Patient: "Nurse, during the operation I heard the doctor say a word that upset me very much."
Nurse: "What was the word?"
Patient: "OOPS!"

SEEING STRAIGHT

Why did the computer go to the optometrist?
To improve its web *sight*!

Javier made an appointment to see a
new optometrist. "Doctor," he said,
"I think I'm suffering from poor eyesight."
"Don't worry," replied the doctor. "I can print your bill larger!"

Eye Doctor: "How many lines can you read on the chart?"
Patient: "What chart?"

Optometrist: "You need new glasses."
Brent: "How do you know? I haven't
even told you what's wrong with me yet."
Optometrist: "I could tell as soon as
you walked in through the window!"

Steve: "I went to the optometrist because I saw
fuzzy spots in front of my eyes. She gave me glasses."
Carol: "Did the glasses help?"
Steve: "Yes. I see the spots clearly now!"

19

THE DRILL TEAM

Why did the pie crust go to the dentist?
It needed a *filling*!

What two letters of the alphabet spell big trouble for your teeth?
D.K.

What did the dentist want from the lawyer?
The tooth, the whole tooth, and nothing but the tooth!

What does a dentist call his X-rays?
Tooth-*pics*!

Drill Sergeant
Army Dentist

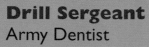

What did the dentist say to the golfer?
"You have a hole in one!"

Why do dentists get fat?
Just about everything they do is *filling*!

What happened when the dentist and the manicurist had an argument?
They fought tooth and nail!

Why did the vampire go to the orthodontist?
To improve his bite!

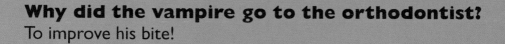

"Doctor, I have yellow teeth. What should I do?"
"Wear a brown tie!"

Why do people dislike going to the dentist?
She's bor-ing!

What did the child say when the dentist asked him what kind of filling he wanted?
Chocolate cream!

21

Dentist: "Please stop howling. I haven't even touched your tooth yet."

Tanya: "I know, but you're standing on my foot!"

What has teeth but never goes to the dentist?
A comb!

What should you do when your tooth falls out?
Quickly get the toothpaste!

Dentist's Motto –
"Easy gum, easy go."

Dave: "I went to the dentist this morning for my toothache."

Gail: "Does your tooth still hurt?"

Dave: "I don't know – the dentist kept it!"

Why did the king go to the dentist?
To get his teeth *crowned*!

What did the tooth say to the dentist as he was leaving?
Fill me in when you get back!

What does the 'Dentist of the Year' get?
A little *plaque*!

What do explorers call it when they go searching for fossil teeth?
A molar expedition!

What time will it be if you miss your dental checkup?
Tooth-hurty!

Why did the tree go to the dentist?
To get a root canal!

Dentist: "I'll pull your aching tooth out in 5 minutes."
George: "How much will it cost?"
Dentist: "$100."
George: "That much for just 5 minutes?"
Dentist: "Well, if you prefer, I can pull it out very slowly."

WRITING JOKES CAN BE AS MUCH FUN AS READING THEM!

Brain teasers are jokes that make you think a little more. They are made to be harder to figure out on purpose. But if you ask a question in a different way, then even the most obvious of answers can be difficult to come by. Here is an example from page 15:

Two girls were born in the same hospital on the same day.
They have the same father and mother, but they are not twins. How can this be?

Answer: They are two of a set of triplets!

This is funny, because the answer seems logical after you hear it. But the joke gives you so many details to think about, that you can't help but laugh at how simple the answer actually is.

YOU TRY IT!

It can be fun to get stumped by a brain teaser, but it's even more fun to stump someone else with one of your own. To do this, it's easiest to start with your answer. So to begin, write down an object or a thing such as a car.

Now, just list some descriptions of this item. Try to avoid making the descriptions too obvious, though. For instance, saying that you drive it is true. But that would make it too easy for someone to figure out your answer. A good description would be:

It can run for hours and not go anywhere.

This description is true, but a car may not be the first thing that comes to mind when hearing it. This is because it can also refer to a lot of other things besides a car.

Brain teasers can be written about almost anything. Try writing some of your own and have fun teasing the brains of your family and friends!

SEND US YOUR JOKES!

Pick out the best brain teaser that you created and send it to us at Norwood House Press. We will publish it on our website — organized according to grade level, the state you live in, and your first name.

Selected jokes might also appear in a future special edition book, *Kids Write in the Funny Zone*. If your joke is included in the book, you and your school will receive a free copy.

Here's how to send the jokes to Norwood House Press:

1) Go to www.norwoodhousepress.com.
2) Click on the **Enter the Funny Zone** tab.
3) Select and print the joke submission form.
4) Fill out the form, include your joke, and send to:
   The Funny Zone
   Norwood House Press
   PO Box 316598
   Chicago, IL 60631

Here's how to see your joke posted on the website:

1) Go to www.norwoodhousepress.com.
2) Click on the **Enter the Funny Zone** tab.
3) Select **Kids Write in the Funny Zone** tab.
4) Locate your grade level, then state, then first name.
   If it's not there yet check back again.